SPANISH 1
LIFEPAC TWO

CONTENTS

Author: **Vicki Seeley Milunich, B.A., M.S. Ed.**
Editor: Alan Christopherson, M.S.
Graphic Design: Kyle Bennett, Jennifer Davis, Alpha Omega Staff

Alpha Omega Publications

Published by Alpha Omega Publications, Inc.
300 North McKemy Avenue, Chandler, Arizona 85226-2618

SPANISH 1: LIFEPAC 2
EN LA ESCUELA

OBJECTIVES

When you have completed this LIFEPAC, you should be able to:

1. Introduce vocabulary relating to school, including the classroom, subjects, **-ar** action verbs and numbers 1–10.

2. Explain the concept of "person" and subject pronouns.

3. Explain the conjugations of **-ar** verbs.

4. Practice basic sentence construction, including saying "not."

5. Explain the basic yes/no question format using inversion and "added" words.

6. Introduce the geographical regions of Mexico.

7. Practice pronunciation and increase speaking simple Spanish sentences.

8. Increase the ability to ask and answer basic yes/no questions.

I. CLASSROOM OBJECTS & NUMBERS

Classroom Objects

la bandera	the flag
el bolígrafo	the pen (ballpoint)
el borrador	the eraser
el cartel	the poster
la cinta	the tape
la computadora	the computer
el cuaderno	the notebook
el diccionario	the dictionary
el escritorio	the desk
el/la estudiante	the student (male/female)
la goma	the pencil eraser
el lápiz	the pencil
el libro	the book
el mapa	the map
la mesa	the table
la mochila	the backpack
el papel	the paper
la pluma	the pen
el profesor	the teacher (male)
la profesora	the teacher (female)
la pizarra	the blackboard
la pupitre	the student desk
la regla	the ruler
el sacapuntas	the pencil sharpener
la silla	the chair
la tiza	the chalk

PICTURE 1

PICTURE 2

 Ejercicio.

1.1   Identify the numbered items in each picture – first in English, then in Spanish.

Picture 1

1. _____   6. _____

2. _____   7. _____

3. _____   8. _____

4. _____   9. _____

5. _____   10. _____

Picture 2

1. _____   6. _____

2. _____   7. _____

3. _____   8. _____

4. _____   9. _____

5. _____   10. _____

3

NUMBERS 1–10

Look at the following pictures and the number they represent.

1. un lápiz y una pluma
2. dos mochilas
3. tres estudiantes

4. cuatro carteles
5. cinco pupitres
6. seis libros

  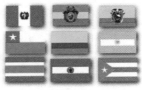

7. siete cuadernos
8. ocho cintas
9. nueve banderas

10. diez sillas

 Practice the following numbers.

1.2   Repeat these numbers, saying them in groups of two, then three, four and five. Repeat them backwards, then odd and even. Look at things around the room and say how many there are of each.

1. one   **uno** – masculine (shortened to **un** before a noun) **una** – feminine ("one" has a gender difference)
2. two: **dos**
3. three: **tres**
4. four: **cuatro**
5. five: **cinco**
6. six: **seis**
7. seven: **siete**
8. eight: **ocho**
9. nine: **nueve**
10. ten: **diez**

DOS.

 Adult check _____

Initial   Date

> **Ejercicio.**

1.3   Label the following pictures, including the quantity of each object.

a._____   b. _____   c. _____

d. _____   e._____   f. _____

g. _____   h. _____   i. _____

j. _____

> **Ejercicio.**

1.4   Write out the following math problems. The math terms are **y** for "and," **menos** for "minus,"
           son for "equals." **For example:** 3 + 4 = 7 would be written: **tres y cuatro son siete.**

           a. 3 + 5 = 8 ___tresy Cienco son ocho_____

           b. 2 + 7 = 9 _____

           c. 10 – 4 = 6 _____

           d. 9 – 1 = 8 _____

           e. 3 + 7 = 10_____

f. 4 + 5 = 9 _____

g. 6 − 2 = 4 _____

h. 1 + 7 = 8 _____

i. 5 + 1 = 6 _____

j. 8 − 4 = 4 _____

 Ejercicio.

1.5 Look at the following pictures and tell your teacher or learning partner **how many of what** are in the picture. The word **hay** means "there is" or "there are."

Example:

Hay dos profesores.

a.

b.

c.

d.

e.

✔ Adult check _____

Initial   Date

SELF TEST 1

1.01 **Look carefully at the following classroom scene and identify the lettered items. Please include the number of items there are.** (3 pts. per number, 3 pts. per item)

a. _____   f. _____

b. _____   g. _____

c. _____   h. _____

d. _____   i. _____

e. _____   j. _____

1.02 **Write out the following math problems.** (10 pts. each question: 2 pts. for each number, and 2 pts. each math function)

    a. 2 + 6 = 8 _____

    b. 3 + 7 = 10 _____

    c. 5 + 4 = 9 _____

1.03   **Identify these pictures.** (2 pts. each)

a.   b.    c.

d.    e.

a. _____

b. _____

c. _____

d. _____

e. _____

Score   _____

Adult check   _____
                  Initial   Date

II. EN LA CLASE DE ESPAÑOL

Listen to/read the conversation between Alicia and Daniel before their history class.

Alicia:	¡Hola, Daniel! ¿Cómo estás?
Daniel:	Bien, gracias. ¿Y tú?
Alicia:	Así, así. ¿Estudias para el examen de español?
Daniel:	Sí. Siempre estudio mucho. Necesito una buena nota.
Alicia:	Yo también. ¿Deseas practicar conmigo?
Daniel:	¡Claro! Vamos a estudiar juntos.
Alicia:	Hello, Daniel. How are you?
Daniel:	Fine, thanks. And you?
Alicia:	So, so. Are you studying for the Spanish exam?
Daniel:	Yes. I always study a lot. I need a good grade.
Alicia:	Me, too. Do you want to practice with me?
Daniel:	Of course. Let's study together.

Ejercicio.

2.1   Practice the above dialogue with your learning partner. Then recite it for your teacher.

✔ Adult check _____

Initial   Date

Rewrite the dialogue, replacing the bolded words with new ones from this vocabulary and the vocabulary of Chapter 1.

2.2

Alicia:	¡**Hola**, Daniel! ¿Cómo estás?
Daniel:	**Bien**, gracias. ¿Y tú?
Alicia:	**Así, así**. ¿Estudias para el examen de **español**?
Daniel:	Sí. Siempre estudio mucho. Necesito una buena nota.
Alicia:	Yo también. ¿Deseas **practicar** conmigo?
Daniel:	¡Claro! Vamos a **estudiar** juntos.

Alicia:	¡_____ , Daniel! ¿Cómo estás?
Daniel:	_____ , gracias. ¿Y tú?
Alicia:	_____ . ¿Estudias para el examen de _____ ?
Daniel:	Sí. Siempre estudio mucho. Necesito una buena nota.
Alicia:	Yo también. ¿Deseas _____ conmigo?
Daniel:	¡Claro! Vamos a _____ juntos.

SELF TEST 2

Complete the dialogue with the letter of the correct word or phrase. (20 pts. each)

2.01   Ana: ¡ _____ , David! ¿Cómo estás?
    a. Bueno   b. Buenos días   c. Adios   d. Hasta la vista

2.02   David: ¡Hola, Ana! Muy bien, ¿Y _____ ?
    a. tú   b. usted

2.03   Ana: Bien. ¿Estudias para el _____ de ciencia?
    a. libro   b. diccionario   c. examen   d. sacapuntas

2.04   David: Sí, deseo _____ bien.
    a. pasar   b. visitar   c. entrar

2.05   Ana: Muy bien. Deseo estudiar _____ .
    a. la silla   b. la bandera   c. la historia   d. la mochila

80 / 100	Score _____
	Teacher check _____
	Initial Date

III. SUBJECT PRONOUNS

Subject pronouns are the words that indicate who is doing the action of a verb. The basic Spanish subject pronouns are:

Person:	Singular:			Plural:	
1st	**yo**	(I)		**nosotros**	(we)
2nd	**tú**	(you, informal)		**vosotros**	(you, informal, Spain only)
3rd	**él**	(he)		**ellos**	(they, masculine or masculine & feminine)
3rd	**ella**	(she)		**ellas**	(they, feminine only)
3rd	**usted**	(you, formal)		**ustedes**	(you)

These are used to help you in your verb conjugations (changing the verb form to indicate who is doing the action). Remember the accent on **él**. Also, when your group of "we" is all female, you use **nosotras** instead of **nosotros**.

"Person" refers to the distinction between the speaker and the persons they are talking to or about. First person always refers to him/herself (I) in the singular and we in the plural. The second person refers to you (informal) and the third person refers to he, she, and you formal in the singular, and they or you, plural, in the plural.

You

Note that there are four ways to say "you" in Spanish in Spain and three ways in the rest of the Spanish- speaking world:

Tú is used when you are talking to one person who is a friend, family member as well as with your pets (familiar).

Usted, often abbreviated **Ud.**, is used when you are addressing someone you should show respect, for example, your pastor, your teachers, your principal, the president, generally most adults other than family members (formal).

Vosotros, used in Spain only, is used to refer to a group of friends or family members. It is the plural of **tú**.

Ustedes, often abbreviated **Uds.**, is used in Spain for the plural formal form, but in the rest of the Spanish-speaking world there is no difference between formal and informal in the plural form.

In these LIFEPACs we will follow the latter and use the **Ustedes** "you" plural form of address in the plural, unless otherwise indicated. The **vosotros** form will always be given for information only.

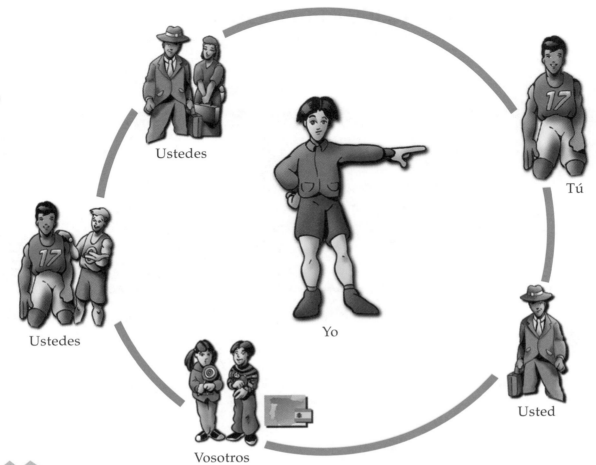

Ejercicio.

3.1   How would you address the following people?

a. a friend _____   f. Sr. Gomez_____

b. your sisters _____   g. Sr. and Sra. Chavez _____

c. Sra. Calderon _____   h. your brother _____

d. your teachers _____   i. your friends _____

e. your cat_____   j. your pastor _____

Ejercicio.

3.2   Ask the following people how they are. Remember to use the proper address. Use one of the following, **¿Cómo estás? ¿Cómo está Ud.?** or **¿Cómo están Uds.?**

a. Sra. Calderón_____

b. Los profesores_____

c. Rafael _____

d. Mamá _____

e. Paco y Mariana_____

SELF TEST 3

3.01　**Which form of "you" would you use with the following people?** (5 pts. each)

a.　Sra. Montoya _____

b.　Michael _____

c.　your friends _____

d.　Sr. and Sra. Gomez _____

e.　your pastor _____

f.　your younger sibling _____

g.　your teacher _____

h.　your dog _____

i.　your classmates _____

j.　a classmate _____

3.02　**Which subject pronoun would you use to represent the following people?** (5 pts. each)

a.　yourself _____

b.　Thomas _____

c.　Mr. Salinas _____

d.　your friends (male) _____

e.　you and a friend _____

f.　a friend to whom you are talking _____

g.　your friends (female) _____

h.　an unknown adult to whom you are talking _____

i.　friends to whom you are talking _____

j.　María _____

$$\frac{80}{100}$$

Score _____

Adult check _____

　　　　　　　　　Initial　　　　　　Date

IV. VERB CONJUGATION

When verbs are conjugated, it means that the verb forms are changed according to whomever is doing the action. In Spanish this is done by changing the ending of the verb. In the dictionaries and in the LIFEPACs, all verbs will be given in the infinitive form. The infinitive is the "to + action" form of the verb. In Spanish there are three conjugations of verbs: **-ar, -er, -ir**.

The first conjugation of verbs is the **-ar** verbs. This means that these verbs end in **-ar** in their "infinitive" form. The infinitive is translated as "to + the action of the verb." For example: **hablar** means "to speak," **cantar** means "to sing" and **pasar** means "to pass." In **hablar** the **habl-** means "speak, without a person speaking," and the **-ar** means "to." When you conjugate a verb you drop the **-ar** which leaves you with the "stem." Then you add a different "ending," depending upon who is doing the action. Look at the following pattern:

hablar – to speak

yo	habl**o**	nosotros	habl**amos**
tú	habl**as**	vosotros	habl**áis** (used in Spain only.)
él	habl**a**	ellos	habl**an**
ella	habl**a**	ellas	habl**an**
usted	habl**a**	ustedes	habl**an**

Notice that the endings change according to whom is speaking. If **yo** (I) am speaking, an **o** is necessary; but if **nosotros** (we) are speaking, **-amos** is added to the stem. Be careful to always match your ending to the person doing the action.

 Conjugate the following verbs using the format above.

4.1 **bailar –** to dance

    a. yo_____   f. nosotros _____

    b. tú _____   g. vosotros_____

    c. él_____   h. ellos_____

    d. ella_____   i. ellas_____

    e. usted_____   j. ustedes _____

4.2 **llegar –** to arrive

    a. yo_____   f. nosotros _____

    b. tú _____   g. vosotros_____

    c. él_____   h. ellos_____

    d. ella_____   i. ellas_____

    e. usted_____   j. ustedes _____

4.3   **mirar** – to watch

         a. yo _____   f. nosotros _____

         b. tú _____   g. vosotros _____

         c. él_____   h. ellos_____

         d. ella_____   i. ellas_____

         e. usted_____   j. ustedes _____

4.4   **buscar** – to look for

         a. yo_____   f. nosotros _____

         b. tú _____   g. vosotros_____

         c. él _____   h. ellos_____

         d. ella_____   i. ellas_____

         e. usted_____   j. ustedes _____

Translations

When you translate these verbs to English you have three ways to translate:

         yo hablo translates to: I speak, I do speak, I am speaking

There are no special helping verbs like *am*, *is*, *are*, *do*, or *does* in Spanish. These verbs are "built into" the verb form.

         Yo busco says: I look for, I do look for, I am looking for

To determine which translation works best for you, say your English sentence out loud using each of the three translations and decide which one fits best. For example: **Yo miro la televisión** can say, "I watch TV", "I am watching TV," or "I do watch TV." But if I add other words to the sentence, only one or two may sound correct. **Yo miro la televisión cada noche a las ocho**. "I watch TV every night at eight" sounds better than "I am watching TV every night at eight." But if a friend asks me what I am doing, I would want the "I am watching TV" instead of the other two.

Translate the following verb forms three ways.

4.5   a. yo llego_____

         b. tú hablas _____

         c. él mira _____

         d. ella baila _____

         e. Usted busca _____

         f. nosotros llegamos _____

         g. vosotros miráis _____

         h. ellos bailan _____

i. ellas buscan _____

j. Ustedes hablan _____

Some other common **ar** verbs are:

ayudar – to help	**llevar** – to carry, to take, to wear
bajar – to go down, lower	**necesitar** – to need
caminar – to walk	**pagar** – to pay
cantar – to sing	**pasar** – to pass
comprar – to buy	**preguntar** – to ask
contestar – to answer	**preparar** – to prepare
cortar – to cut	**regresar** – to return
desear – to wish	**sacar (fotos)** – to take (pictures)
enseñar – to teach	**terminar** – to finish, to end
entrar – to enter	**tomar** – to take: to have (food/drink)
escuchar – to listen to	**trabajar** – to work
estudiar – to study	**viajar** – to travel
explicar – to explain	**visitar** – to visit

Study Hint: Look at the verbs **entrar**, **pasar**, **preparar** and **visitar**. From Section One do you remember what these type of words are called?

Look at the verbs **cantar, desear**, and **terminar**. What synonym in English would help you remember each of these?

Remember to try to make a system of relationships to help you increase your Spanish vocabulary.

Suggested activities.

4.6

a. Take four or five of the new vocabulary verbs and conjugate them in your notebook or on the board.

b. Make flashcards using pictures or drawings indicating the meanings of 10–15 of these verbs and use them to study.

c. Try to act out one of the actions and have your classmates tell which action you are doing.

 Adult check _____

Initial   Date

Fill in the blank with the correct form of the verb in parentheses and then give the English meaning.

4.7
    a. Yo _____ (cortar) _____

    b. Ellos _____ (pagar) _____

    c. Tú _____ (ayudar) _____

    d. Ustedes _____ (comprar) _____

    e. Ella _____ (estudiar) _____

    f. Nosotros _____ (visitar) _____

    g. Él _____ (necesitar) _____

    h. Vosotros _____ (tomar) _____

    i. Usted _____ (caminar) _____

    j. Ellas _____ (viajar) _____

Christina

Pablo

Ana y Luisa

Marco y Tomás

Explanation

When using verbs, your subject may not always be a specific pronoun. It may be a person's name, another noun or a title. To determine which form of the verb to use, you use the form that matches the pronoun that could replace that subject. For example, if I wanted to say "Matthew teaches," I know that instead of Matthew, I could use "he." Therefore, I need the **él** form of the verb to come up with **Mateo** (Spanish for Matthew) **enseña**. This also happens in the **nosotros** form when the subject of your sentence is someone and I. **Luisa y yo** or **tú y yo** indicate that the **nosotros** form of the verb is necessary.

 Following this concept, decide which subject pronoun could replace the following subjects.

4.8
    a. Maria _____

    b. Luis _____

    c. Elisa y Ana _____

    d. Sr. Lopez _____

    e. Dr. Avila _____

    f. Paco y yo _____

    g. Tomás y Roberto _____

    h. Sra. Gomez _____

    i. Los chicos _____

    j. Sra. Jimenez y yo _____

Ejercicio.

4.9   Complete the following with the correct form of the verb in parentheses at the end of the sentence and then translate it **one** of the three ways.

a. Yo _____ (bailar)   _____

b. Mariana _____ (estudiar)   _____

c. Arturo y yo _____ (hablar)   _____

d. Tú _____ (preparar)   _____

e. Las chicas _____ (llegar)   _____

f. El Sr. Lopez _____ (pagar)   _____

g. Tú y yo_____ (entrar)   _____

h. Paco y Victor _____ (ayudar)   _____

i. Los señores_____ (escuchar)   _____

j. Ustedes_____ (viajar)   _____

SELF TEST 4

4.01 **Fill in the blank with the correct form of the verb in parentheses.** (4 pts. each)

a. Paco _____ el español. (estudiar)

b. Nosotros _____ los libros. (tomar)

c. Ud. _____ la música. (escuchar)

d. Tú _____ la historia. (preparar)

e. Yo _____ el diccionario. (llevar)

f. Francisco y Luis _____ bien. (cantar)

g. Nosotros _____ visitar el museo. (desear)

h. Uds. _____ el francés. (practicar)

i. Ana _____ a Pablo. (ayudar)

j. Pilar y Laura _____ la pizarra. (mirar)

4.02 **Translate the following verb forms three ways.** (20 pts. for this exercise)

a. visito _____

b. preparamos _____

c. entras _____

4.03 **Give the English translation for the following words.** (4 pts. each)

a. terminar _____

b. llegar _____

c. mirar _____

d. explicar _____

e. contestar _____

f. tomar _____

g. trabajar _____

h. hablar _____

i. cantar _____

j. estudiar _____

$\dfrac{80}{100}$

Score _____

Adult check _____
　　　　　　　　Initial　　　　　　Date

V. BASIC SENTENCE STRUCTURE

Conversation

  Listen to and repeat the following conversation.

5.1   Alicia: Daniel, yo necesito un lápiz. Yo contesto las preguntas de matemáticas.

Daniel: Llevo dos lápices. Tú tomas uno.

Alicia: Gracias. ¿Estudias tú la historia?

Daniel: No, yo no estudio la historia. Yo miro la lección de inglés.

Alicia: Yo termino las matemáticas y entonces, yo preparo la lección de química.

✔ Adult check _____
                        Initial   Date

  Answer the following true/false questions concerning the above conversation.
Write V for verdadero (true) and F for falso (false).

5.2   a. _____ Daniel necesita un lápiz.

b. _____ Daniel lleva dos lápices.

c. _____ Alicia estudia matemáticas.

d. _____ Daniel mira la lección de historia.

e. _____ Alicia prepara la lección de química.

  Suggested activities.

5.3   a. Practice the dialogue, memorize it and say it to your teacher.

b. Redo the dialogue, replacing all the nouns with different nouns; i.e., a different subject or object.

✔ Adult check _____
                        Initial   Date

Basic Sentence Structure

In Spanish—just as in English—there may be variations in word order. For example, in English we may say "Tomorrow I am studying for my history test" or we may say "I am studying for my history test tomorrow." Or "tomorrow" may come between "studying" and "for." We manage to keep certain groups of words together, but their placement may vary in our sentences. In this sentence we would never break up "I am studying" or "for my history test."

This happens in Spanish as well, but there is greater variation. For the most part a simple sentence will be formed by using a subject (if necessary), a verb conjugated to go with the subject, and any other pertinent information. For example:

(Yo) preparo la lección de inglés.	I prepare the English lesson.
(Nosotros) viajamos a España.	We are visiting Spain.
Paco contesta la problema de mátematicas.	Paco answers the math problem.

Note that the **yo** and **nosotros** are in parentheses as they are not necessary because the end of the verb indicates who is doing the action. You may choose to use them or not. It may be easier to include them until you are comfortable with the process.

Negative Sentences

To make a sentence negative using "not," place a **no** directly in front of the verb. For example:

Luis no practica el francés	Luis doesn't practice French.
Los chicos no contestan.	The boys do not answer.
Yo no canto bien.	I don't sing well.
Tú no llevas los libros.	You are not carrying the books.
Ana y yo no regresamos.	Ann and I are not returning.

Notice in the negative that the "helping" verbs (do, does, am, is, are) are used in English but not in Spanish.

Rewrite the following sentences in the negative by placing the "no" in the correct place.

5.4

a. Teresa monta la bicicleta. _____

b. Miguel regresa a la escuela. _____

c. Yo pregunto la pregunta. _____

d. Nosotros ayudamos a Roberto. _____

e. Tú compras dos cuadernos. _____

f. Los estudiantes estudian el francés. _____

g. Usted necesita un libro. _____

h. Las profesoras explican la lección. _____

i. Ustedes trabajan mucho. _____

j. Yo termino el ejercicio. _____

When answering questions in the negative, you may use **no** twice. The first **no** responds to the question, and the second **no** makes the verb negative (not). For example:

¿Terminas tú la literatura?	No, yo no termino la literatura.
Are you finishing the literature?	No, I am not finishing the literature.
¿Prepara Miguel la música?	No, Miguel no prepara la música.
Is Michael preparing the music?	No, Michael is not preparing the music.

Answer the following questions in the negative.

5.5   Make sure to respond with the appropriate person for the answer. If the question is asked of you (**tú** or **usted**) you answer with **yo**. If **vosotros** or **ustedes** is used, answer with **nosotros**. If you are asking about someone (**él, ella, ellos, ellas**) then use the same form.

a   ¿Habla Luis francés? _____

b. ¿Escuchas tú la música? _____

c. ¿Llevan los chico los libros? _____

d. ¿Visitan Uds. el museo? _____

e. ¿Toma Ud. el diccionario? _____

Questions

There are three ways to form questions that would be answered with yes or no (**Sí** or **no**).

The first way is **inversion**. This means that the subject and verb of the sentence are inverted (switch places). For example:

> **Paco viaja a Mexico becomes ¿Viaja Paco a Mexico?**
>
> Paco travels to Mexico – Does Paco travel to Mexico? *or* Is Paco travelling to Mexico?
>
> **Tú caminas a la escuela. becomes ¿Caminas tú a la escuela?**
>
> You walk to school – Do you walk to school? *or* Are you walking to school?

Look at the way that **Paco viaja** now is **Viaja Paco** with the proper punctuation – ¿ ?. And **tú caminas** becomes **Caminas tú**. This is inversion.

Notice also again the use of the "built-in" helping words in the English translation.

Ejercicio.

5.6

Rewrite the following statements in question form using inversion.

a. Diana necesita una pluma. _____

b. Tú pasas el inglés. _____

c. Los chicos visitan a un amigo. _____

d. Yo contesto la pregunta. _____

e. Ustedes entran en la clase. _____

f. Nts. miramos la televisión. _____

g. Usted termina la lección. _____

h. David saca fotos. _____

i. La profesora enseña español. _____

j. Susana y Carlos estudian. _____

Ejercicio.

5.7

Translate the questions you have made to English. You may use either group of helping verbs do/does or am/is/are.

a. _____

b. _____

c. _____

d. _____

e. _____

f. _____

g. _____

h. _____

i. _____

j. _____

The second and third way to make a question with a yes/no answer is to add either **¿no?** or **¿verdad?** to the end of the statement. These are translated as "right?" or "doesn't/isn't he/she/it?"

For example:

Micaela desea estudiar, ¿no?	Michelle wishes to study, right?
Luis trabaja en casa, ¿verdad?	Luis works at home, doesn't he?
Ustedes hablan español, ¿no?	You speak Spanish, don't you?
Nosotros no regresamos, ¿verdad?	We are not returning, right?

 Ejercicio.

5.8   Make the following statements into questions using either **¿no?** or **¿verdad?**

a. Graciela prepara la lección._____

b. Yo explico la pregunta. _____

c. Tú cortas el papel. _____

d. Ernesto y yo compramos los lápices. _____

e. Ustedes escuchan bien. _____

Oral Practice.

5.9   Respond orally in the negative to the following questions.

    a. ¿Necesita Ud. un lápiz?

    b. ¿Miras la televisión?

    c. ¿Regresan Pablo y Nicolás?

    d. ¿Explica la profesora la pregunta?

    e. ¿Buscan Uds. las mochilas?

✔ Adult check _____
                                     Initial   Date

Conversation.

5.10   Use your vocabulary list to help you create this directed dialogue with your learning partner.

A. Ask a friend if he is looking for something.

B. Respond that you are not looking for that object.

A. Ask him if he is looking for another object.

B. Respond that you are.

A. Respond that you wish to help.

B. Thank him.

✔ Adult check _____
                                     Initial   Date

SELF TEST 5

5.01 **Rewrite the following statements into yes/no questions using inversion.** (5 pts. each)

    a. Raúl estudia la biología._____

    b. Ud. canta la música bien._____

    c. Tomás y Carmen practican mucho._____

    d. Lucia termina la historia._____

    e. Tú enseñas la química. _____

5.02 **Rewrite the following statements into yes/no questions using ¿no?** (5 pts. each)

    a. Jorge desea regresar. _____

    b. Edmundo busca el libro. _____

    c. Nosotros terminamos la ciencia. _____

    d. Yo explico las matemáticas. _____

    e. Tú necesitas un lápiz. _____

5.03 **Rewrite the following statements into yes/no questions using ¿verdad?** (5 pts. each)

    a. Eduardo pregunta. _____

    b. Tú sacas fotos._____

    c. Yo contesto la pregunta._____

    d. Nosotros pagamos. _____

    e. Uds. escuchan la música._____

5.04 **Answer the following question negatively.** (5 pts. each)

    a. ¿Preparas tú la historia?_____

    b. ¿Enseña la profesora la biblia? _____

    c. ¿Visitan Uds. la clase?_____

    d. ¿Necesita Ud. una pluma? _____

    e. ¿Regresan Daniel y David?_____

$\dfrac{80}{100}$

Score   _____

Adult check   _____

                             Initial   Date

VI. SPEAKING, WRITING, AND READING PRACTICE

Let's Speak

Create your own conversation using the cues indicated.

6.1   The situation is that you walk into the classroom and see your friend.

A. Greet your friend.

B. Respond.

A. Ask if (s)he wishes to study a certain subject.

B. Respond negatively.

A. Ask her/him to explain a subject.

B. Respond positively.

A. Thank her/him.

B. Respond appropriately.

✔ Adult check _____

Initial   Date

Pronunciation Pointers

The letters r and rr.

The letter **r** is pronounced in almost the same manner that we do in English when it is placed in the middle or end of a word. However, if it begins the word or is doubled (**rr**), then it has a "trill" to it. To do this, take your tongue and tap it up and down two or three times against the ridge behind the upper teeth. Practice with the following words:

Raquel	carro (caro)	aburrido (bored)
Rosalia	perro (dog)	gorra (cap)
Ramón	corre (he runs)	ropa (clothes)

After the consonants **l, n** or **s**, the single **r** is also trilled.

honra (honor)   Israel   alrededor

Keep in mind the double **r** sound because there are words that have similar spelling but have double **r** or single **r**:

caro – expensive   **carro** – car

pero – but   **perro** – dog

Listen carefully and try to imitate the sounds.

Listen to the tape, or your teacher will dictate the above four words. Write each word in the order you hear it.

6.2   a._____   c._____.

         b._____   d. _____

Listen to the list of words. Next to the letter write one (1) if you hear one r or two (2) if you hear the trilled r. (You may wish to write the word you hear on the blank.)

6.3   a._____   f. _____

         b._____   g. _____

         c._____   h. _____

         d._____   i. _____

         e._____   j. _____

Listen to the questions and answer them.

6.4   a. _____

         b. _____

         c. _____

         d. _____

         e. _____

1.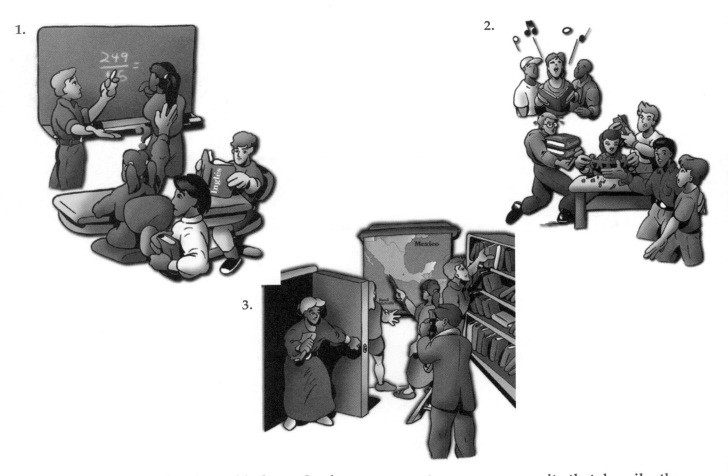

2.

3.

Look at the picture(s) above. See how many sentences you can write that describe the actions going on in the pictures. Using your vocabulary list and the name list, give the characters names and describe what they are doing.

6.5 _____

_____

_____

_____

_____

_____

_____

_____

_____

_____

_____

_____

_____

_____

_____

Let's Read

Read the following paragraph and answer the questions after it.

Alicia y Daniel llegan a la clase de inglés. Alicia necesita un cuaderno. Daniel necesita un bolígrafo. Miran en las mochilas. Toman el cuaderno y el bolígrafo. Estudian un párrafo de inglés. Buscan palabras semejantes a español. Las palabras ayudan a Alicia y a Daniel estudiar. La profesora explica la lección de hoy. Necesitan hablar dos o tres minutos en inglés. Necesitan practicar mucho. Alicia y Daniel trabajan diez minutos. Entonces, hablan con la profesora. La profesora escucha con interés. Preparan bien. Finalmente terminan. Solamente usan el diccionario un poco.

Vocabulario

un párrafo – a paragraph
las palabras – the words
semejante – similar
de hoy – for today
un minuto – a minute

entonces – then
con interés – with interest
finalmente – finally
solamente – only

 Verdadero o falso. Write V **for verdadero (true) and** F **for falso (false).**

6.6

1. _____ Alicia y Daniel estudian inglés.

2. _____ No necesitan nada (nothing).

3. _____ Toman una regla de la mochila.

4. _____ Usan español para ayudar.

5. _____ Daniel explica la lección.

6. _____ Necesitan hablar dos minutos.

7. _____ Practican mucho.

8. _____ La profesora no escucha.

9. _____ No preparan bien.

10. _____ Usan el diccionario.

Note: This section does not have a Self Test

VII. THE GEOGRAPHY OF MEXICO

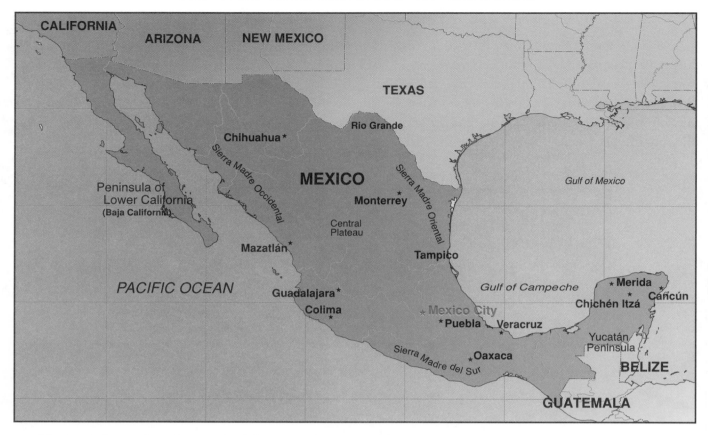

Mexico is located to the south of the United States. It shares borders with Texas, New Mexico, Arizona and California. Part of this border is formed by the Rio Grande River. Mexico is the fifth largest country of the western hemisphere, encompassing an area about one-quarter the size of the United States. It has a population of approximately 84 million people. Its capital is Mexico City where nearly 20 million people live, making it the largest Spanish-speaking city in the world.

Mexico's geography is extremely varied. In the northwest is the peninsula of Lower California (Baja California) while to the southeast is the Yucatán Peninsula. In between there is the Sierra Madre mountain range which is divided into three ranges: Sierra Madre Oriental to the east, Sierra Madre Occidental to the west and Sierra Madre del Sur to the south. In between the Oriental and Occidental is the Central Plateau (Meseta de Anáhuac).

Along the western coast are the resort communities of Mazatlán and Colima. Along the eastern shore are the important ports of Veracruz and Tampico. The Yucatán Peninsula is home to Cancun, Merida and Chichén-Itzá. This area is especially known for its Mayan ruins.

In the interior is the capital and the important cities of Puebla, Guadalajara (second largest city in Mexico), Oaxaca, Monterrey, Taxco (know for its colonial appearance) and Chihuahua.

The southern border of Mexico is shared with Guatemala, another Spanish-speaking country, and Belize, the only English-speaking country in Central America.

The aqueous boundaries include the Pacific Ocean to the west and to the east the Gulf of Campeche and the Gulf of Mexico.

Mexico City, D.F. (Distrito Federal), the capital of Mexico, lies on the remains of the ancient Aztec Indian capital, Tenochtitlán, which is on Lake Texcoco. This underground lake has posed many construction problems for the city, interfering with the construction of many modern buildings and subways.

Some of the most interesting historical sights in Mexico City are:

1. El Parque Chapultepec where the people can enjoy the zoo and museums such as the castle built by Maximilian that was formerly the presidential residence.

2. El Zócalo, also known as the Plaza Mayor, is the main "square" of the town which houses the municipal and government buildings around it.

3. The Basilica de Guadalupe, the most famous church in Mexico, was built to honor the patron saint of Mexico.

4. Xochimilco is the name of the floating gardens which give a Venice-type air to the area.

5. Paseo de la Reforma is a large boulevard which extends from Chapultepec park through the area, containing the elegant hotels, shops and theaters. At the Paseo's large traffic circles, statues and monuments celebrating Mexico's history can be seen.

 Complete the following activities:

7.1 Draw your own map of Mexico, labeling all the important regions and cities. Put it in your notebook for future reference.

✔ Adult check _____
                        Initial   Date

7.2 Write a letter to one of the following organizations requesting information about Mexico.

Hispanic Mission to the US
Mexico
Two United Nations Plaza, 28th Floor
New York, NY 10017

Mexican Embassy
1911 Pennsylvania Ave. N W
Washington, DC 20006

Mexican Office of Tourism
1911 Pennsylvania Ave. NW
Washington, SC 20006

Mexican Consulate
2827 16th St. NW
Washington, DC 20009-4260

✔ Adult check _____
                        Initial   Date

SELF TEST 7

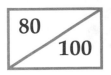

Match the following. (5 pts. each)

7.01

1. _____ The second largest city in Mexico

2. _____ Three ranges of mountains

3. _____ The capital of Mexico and largest Hispanic city in the world.

4. _____ The city known for its colonial appearance.

5. _____ The eastern water border.

6. _____ The area known for the Mayan ruins

7. _____ Two resort communities on the western shore.

8. _____ Two eastern shore ports.

9. _____ The northwest peninsula which shares a name with a U.S. state.

10. _____ The other English speaking border country besides the U.S.

a. Tampico and Veracruz

b. Sierra Madre

c. The Yucatán Peninsula

d. The Gulf of Mexico

e. Mexico City

f. Taxco

g. Guadalajara

h. Mazatlán and Colima

i. Baja California

j. Belize

Answer the following questions about Mexico. (5 pts. each)

7.02 What river forms part of the border between Mexico and the United States?

7.03 How many mountain ranges are there in the Sierra Madre chain? List them.

7.04 What Indian ruins are famous in the Yucatán Peninsula?

7.05 What is the name of the area where the capital is located?

7.06 Name two countries that border Mexico.

7.07 What type of activities do people enjoy in Chapultepec Park in Mexico City?

7.08 What is the Zócalo?

7.09 Who is the patron saint of Mexico?

7.010 What is the name of the street in Mexico City noted for its elegant hotels and shops?

7.011 Name three resort communities or ports in Mexico.

$\frac{80}{100}$

Score _____

Teacher check _____

Initial   Date

34

VIII. REVIEW EXERCISES

Review exercises from Spanish LIFEPAC 2

Look at the following picture and identify the lettered objects.

8.1   a. _____   g. _____

b. _____   h. _____

c. _____   i. _____

d. _____   j. _____

e. _____   k. _____

f. _____

8.2   **Look at the following picture and identify the lettered objects.**

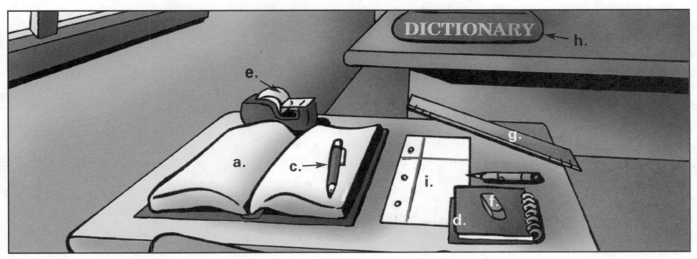

a. _____   f. _____

b. _____   g. _____

c. _____   h. _____

d. _____   i. _____

e. _____

8.3   Fill in the conjugation of the following verbs.

	comprar	viajar	escuchar
yo			
tú			
él			
ella			
Ud.			
nts.			
ellos			
ellas			
Uds.			

8.4   Rewrite the following sentences in question form using inversion. Then answer them in the negative.

a.   Pablo visita la clase de inglés.

b.   Tú miras la pizarra.

c.   Uds. trabajan. en matemáticas.

d.   Los chicos estudian el español.

e.   Yo necesito un lápiz.

Review Exercises from Spanish LIFEPAC 1

 Write out the spelling for the following words.

8.5   a. llevar _____

b. español _____

c. claro _____

d. juntos _____

e pizarra _____

Divide the following words and underline the stressed syllable.

8.6 a. l i t e r a t u r a

 b. p r o f e s o r

 c. c o n t a b i l i d a d

 d. s a c a p u n t a s

 e. e s t u d i a n t e

 What action would you be doing if your teacher said the following?

8.7 a. Abran sus libros. _____

 b. Siéntense _____

 c. Saquen el libro. _____

 d. Repitan _____

 e. Escriban su nombre. _____

 Which form of "you" would you use when talking to the following people?

8.8 a. La Sra. Garcia _____

 b. Pepe _____

 c. los amigos _____

 d. Sr. y Sra. Gomez _____

 e. la madre _____

 Conversational Practice. Complete the following activities.

8.9 Listen and repeat the following conversation.

 Alicia: ¡Hola, Daniel! ¿Cómo estás?
 Daniel: ¡Hola, Alicia! Muy bien, ¿y tú?
 Alicia: ¡Fantástica! ¿Qué estudias?
 Daniel: Estudio la geografía de México.
 Alicia: Yo, también. Estudiamos juntos.
 Daniel: Está bien. ¿Cómo se llaman las montañas?
 Alicia: Sierra Madre, hay tres: Oriental, Occidental y del Sur.
 Daniel: Muy bien.

8.10 Prepare a conversation with your learning partner in which you do the following:
 a. Greet each other and ask how are you?
 b. Ask a question about school.
 c. Respond correctly and ask another question.
 d. Respond correctly.
 e. Make a joint decision.
 f End the conversation.

 Adult check _____
                                    Initial   Date

37

LIFEPAC 2: VOCABULARY LIST

Los verbos:

ayudar	to help
bailar	to dance
bajar	to go down, lower
buscar	to look for
caminar	to walk
cantar	to sing
comprar	to buy
contestar	to answer
cortar	to cut
desear	to wish
enseñar	to teach
entrar (en)	to enter (in)
escuchar	to listen (to)
estudiar	to study
explicar	to explain
hablar	to speak
llegar	to arrive, to reach
llevar	to carry, take, wear
mirar	to look (at)
montar	to ride
necesitar	to need
pagar	to pay
pasar	to pass, to happen
practicar	to practice
preguntar	to ask a question
preparar	to prepare
regresar	to return
sacar (fotos)	to take (pictures)
terminar	to finish
tomar	to take, to have (food)
trabajar	to work
viajar	to travel
usar	to use
visitar	to visit

Other words:

hay	there is/are
juntos	together
también	also
claro	of course
mucho	a lot, much
la nota	the grade
vamos a	let's
hay	there is, there are

Los sustantivos (nouns)

School subjects:

el arte	art
la biblia	bible
la biología	biology
las ciencias	science
la contabilidad	accounting
la educacion física	physical education
el español	Spanish
la física	physics
el francés	French
la geografía	geography
la geometría	geometry
el grado	grade
la historia	history
el inglés	English
la literatura	literature
las matemáticas	mathmatics
la música	music
la nota	the grade (test)
la programación de computadoras	computer programming
la química	chemistry
la religión	religion

Classroom objects:

Spanish	English	Spanish	English
la bandera	the flag	el libro	the book
el bolígrafo	the pen	el mapa	the map
el borrador	the eraser (blackboard)	la mesa	the table
el cartel	the poster	la mochila	the backpack
la cinta	the tape	el papel	the paper
la computadora	the computer	la pluma	the pen
el cuaderno	the notebook	el profesor	the teacher
el diccionario	the dictionary	la pizarra	the blackboard
el escritorio	the desk	la regla	the ruler
el estudiante	the student (male)	el sacapuntas	the pencil sharpener
la estudiante	the student (female)	la silla	the chair
la goma	the pencil eraser	la tiza	the chalk
el lápiz	the pencil		

39